SAN DIEGO *in color*

Text by Catherine Reade
Concept/Design by Nicky Kronick

Published by Ventures International, P.O. Box 6539, San Diego, Ca. 92106

ISBN 0-917437-00-4

OLD TOWN

In a city of high-rise urbanity and suburban sprawl, linked and crossed by four-lane freeways, Old Town offers tree-lined streets, tiny shops and tradition. Here, where the Spanish settled in 1769, you can stroll, shop, dine and explore while absorbing the curious blend of Spanish missionary and Mexican-Indian which is California's rich heritage.

Stepping back into history more than 200 years, we find that San Diego was little more than a magnificent bay surrounded by arid hills. Several explorers had been here before its settlement: Juan Cabrillo discovered the harbor in 1542 naming it San Miguel; and, in 1602, it was rediscovered by Sebastián Vizcaino who renamed it San Diego. Even though Spain laid title to this land there was no attempt to settle it for 167 years after the bay was rediscovered.

This indifference ended in 1769 when the King of Spain, Carlos III, feared losing California to Russia. He rapidly appointed a military and secular expedition to establish a Presidio and mission, firmly claiming the rights of Spain.

Three ships and two land parties were formed. Heading the expedition was Captain de Gaspar Portolá and Father Junípero Serra, a Franciscan friar who would eventually found a chain of 21 missions along California's El Camino Real.

Two of Portolá's ships arrived at their destination in April and May of 1769. The third was lost at sea. Concurrently, the first land party, coming from Baja

continued

California, arrived to find the ship's company camped by the harbor. Land party leader Captain Fernando Rivera y Moncado moved the encampment to what is now Presidio Hill, establishing military headquarters, a hospital and corral.

Father Serra and his land party were the last to reach San Diego on July 1, 1769. Sixteen days after his arrival he founded California's first mission, San Diego de Alcala, and dedicated the Presidio.

During the next 31 years, the Mission and Presidio valiantly survived Indian attacks and water shortages. The Mission was moved to Mission Valley, Indian threats ceased, and colonists in the early 1800's began a settlement at the base of Presidio Hill. This is today's Old Town.

While Old Town grew with homes like Casa de Bandini and Casa de Estudillo, shops and a one-room school, Spain lost control of Mexico making California a Mexican Territory in 1822.

With few exceptions, San Diego's complexion changed very little. Old Town continued to grow. San Diego became the capital of Alta and Baja California for five years beginning in 1825. And the whaling and hide trade made the community prosperous.

After 22 years of Mexican rule, California was surrendered to the United States in 1846. When California became a state in 1850, San Diego became its first county.

Also in 1850 there was an attempt to move Old Town into New Town, a site on the harbor where some of the City Fathers felt San Diego could better develop and prosper. This plan was abortive until 1867 when Alonzo E. Horton, a San Francisco financier, arrived.

Horton, undaunted by past failures, purchased 1000 acres on the waterfront and began enticing merchants and residents with free land. The move to New Town was slow until 1872 when a fire destroyed much of Old Town, forcing residents and merchants to move four miles closer to the harbor.

Old Town today is a mingling of a colorful past with the present. Scattered throughout this six block area is the town's early plaza, a dozen founding homes, the one-room Mason Street school, the original San Diego Union office, and the 1850 cemetery, El Campo Santo. Bazaar Del Mundo, a modern addition to Old Town, is a collection of restaurants and specialty shops that underscore the town's Mexican tradition.

Still standing above Old Town is Presidio Hill. The original fortress and mission have long since fallen into ruins. In their place stands Serra Museum containing many artifacts covering the Spanish and Mexican eras.

HERITAGE PARK

Heritage Park, on a gentle slope overlooking the eastern end of Old Town, is a restoration project of the Save Our Heritage Organization (SOHO). These landmark homes, once threatened by bulldozers in their original neighborhoods, were brought together and now form a charming addition to Old Town.

CABRILLO NATIONAL MONUMENT AND POINT LOMA

Gracing the southern tip of the Point Loma peninsula is a tiny lighthouse. It was built in 1854 to warn merchant ships and whalers of the rocky dangers at the mouth of the San Diego Harbor. Because not easily seen from its 462 foot perch, a new lighthouse was built 36 years later at the base of the peninsula but the original lighthouse, which underwent extensive restoration in the early 1980's, remains as a significant part of the Cabrillo National Monument.

This 144-acre monument commemorates Juan Rodriguez Cabrillo's discovery of California in 1542 and is one of the most visited areas of the National Park System.

From the terrace of the visitor center and the lighthouse, the panorama is spectacular. The bay, open sea, Baja Califorrna and the Coronado Islands are all within view.

A popular annual attraction is the California gray whale migration. Each year between December and February the gray whales swim from the Bering Sea to the lagoons of Mexico to have their young.

Traveling to and from Cabrillo National Monument, you pass through a large military reservation, Fort Rosecrans National Cemetery, and the beautiful community of Point Loma.

Point Loma, like Janus, has two faces: one looks to the bay and the other to the Pacific.

On both sides are palatial homes with striking views. The bay side features Shelter Island with its tropical mixture of restaurants, hotels, yacht brokers and ship chandlers. The ocean side is less developed with craggy cliffs, windswept beaches, and the oldest suburb in San Diego, Ocean Beach.

Sunset Cliffs are ragged from the waves continually carving tunnels and caves into their facade; and, contrastingly, smooth Ocean Beach, with the longest fishing pier on the West Coast, is perfect for picnicking, sunbathing, and building sandcastles.

OCEAN BEACH

SUNSET CLIFFS

THE EMBARCADERO AND BAY

A successful development of prime waterfront land is Seaport Village with its diverse boutiques and restaurants. Combining Victorian, Old Monterey and traditional Spanish architectural styles, the Village has become a popular outing spot for locals and visitors alike.

The lower Embarcadero is currently being expanded by the construction of a world class convention center and major hotels.

Spanning the lower bay, the Coronado Bay Bridge, completed in 1969 at a cost of $50,000,000, provides some spectacular views of the city skyline. With traffic at roughly 16,000,000 cars annually, the bridge is expected to be paid for 16-17 years ahead of its scheduled 2003 due date.

STAR OF INDIA

With sails and decks filled, the Star of India, oldest iron windjammer afloat, proudly led the bicentennial celebration parade of ships through San Diego Harbor, July 4, 1976.

From her launching in 1863, the Star logged 27 circumnavigations of the globe. She flew under three nations' flags during her maritime career. Put out of service in the 1920's, the Star spent many years at anchor before being acquired by the Maritime Museum of San Diego. The ship was first opened to public viewing in 1961, but restoration work is still lovingly carried on. The Star of India shares a birth at the Embarcadero with two other Maritime Museum ships, the ferryboat Berkeley and the steam yacht Media.

DOWNTOWN SAN DIEGO

Only a few years ago San Diego's downtown area was suffering the flight of business to the suburbs, leaving a potentially blighted urban core. A group of San Diegans responded to the situation by committing themselves to the revitalization of the center city. Development of the Community Concourse complex housing the 3000-seat civic auditorium, 5000-seat convention hall, 14 story city administration building and parking garage spurred the business community and resulted in construction of numerous new financial buildings and hotels.

The decade of the 80's is witnessing dynamic growth and change in five areas: Horton Plaza, which includes a major retail shopping center, luxury condos and commercial buildings; the Marina, residential housing; Columbia, a designated mix of cultural and commercial uses; the Gaslamp Quarter, a 16-square block historical restoration and renovation project, and the Embarcadero, with water oriented retail, service and recreational uses, major hotels and the site of the city's new convention center.

The quality of San Diego's growth is reflected by a community that has made a priority of not only maintaining California's second largest city, but keeping it one of America's most beautiful and liveable.

MILITARY

The words "San Diego" and "Navy" have become synonymous in the minds of millions of people over the past half century.

San Diego is the site of major fleet and shore commands, including: Commander, Naval Base, San Diego; Naval Surface Forces and Naval Air Forces, Pacific; and the Marine Corps Camp Pendleton. Shore installations include: Naval Station; North Island Naval Air Station; Amphibious Base; Naval Training Center; Marine Corps Recruit Depot; Naval Ocean Systems Command; Miramar Naval Air Station; Balboa Naval Hospital, and numerous others.

Uniforms change over the years, but the scene is repeated over and over: a sailor, this one from the U.S.S. TARAWA, LHA-1, receives the customary shore-leave greeting from a loved one.

BALBOA PARK

San Diegans have a love affair going with this park — all 1400 acres of it. Time after time, when the temporary buildings of the 1915-16 Panama Exposition began to deteriorate, the citizenry passed new bond issues to preserve and restore them. The Panama Exposition was the beginning of the park and San Diego wants to keep its heritage intact.

Perched in the middle of the park's rolling green lawns are museums, restaurants and theaters. The Prado is the main avenue that connects you with all the parks treasures. Walk down the Prado, view the architectural bouquet of Moorish and Spanish facades in a multi-hued setting of greenery and flowers. See if you don't agree that this is one of the City's stellar attractions.

On your walk you first come to the Museum of Man with its 200-foot landmark tower. Displays of Indian cultures found throughout the Americas are featured here as are frequent live craft demonstrations.

The next complex consists of the Old Globe Theatre, Cassius Carter Center Stage and the outdoor Festival Stage used for summer plays.

San Diego is justly proud of its Museum of Arts and the adjacent Timken Gallery. They contain one of the finest art collections on the West Coast, with emphasis on Spanish, Italian, Flemish, Dutch and Russian art. Only a few of the artists represented include Velásques, Goya, El Greco, Titian, Giorgine, Tintoretto, Rubens, Rembrandt and Van Dyck.

The Sculpture Garden Cafe offers a delightful setting in which to enjoy a light lunch amid 20 works by artists including Marino Marini and Henry Moore.

The Botanical Building, a super-sized lath house containing over 500 varieties of plant life, sits behind a huge lily pond, a favorite park photo spot.

The Natural History Museum features exhibits of local geology and animal life. Also, this 100-year old regional museum has an 88,000 volume scientific library open to the public, a seismograph recording the earths movement and the giant Foucault pendulum illustrating the earths rotation.

Crossing to the south side of El Prado, the Reuben H. Fleet Space Theater and Science Cen-

BALBOA PARK *continued*

ter offers films on the story of the Universe and spectacular travel adventures projected on a dome-shaped Omnimax screen. The seating allows the audience to experience a feeling of participation in the proceedings.

The Casa De Balboa was destroyed by fire in 1978, as was the now rebuilt Old Globe Theatre. The recently restored building now houses the Museum of San Diego History, Model Railroad Museum, the Balboa Art Conservation Center, Museum of Photographic Arts and the San Diego Hall of Champions. The latter honors San Diego athletes including: Florence Chadwick, first woman to successfully swim the English Channel both ways; Maureen Connolly, three-time U.S. and Wimbledon winner; Ted Williams, baseball's immortal .400 hitter; Archie Moore, light-heavyweight title holder, Gene Littler and Billy Casper, U.S. Open golf champions; and Karen Hantze, Wimbledon Champion.

BALBOA PARK *continued*

Next door, the Cafe Del Rey Moro sits in a European garden setting in the House of Hospitality.

Across the square is the Art Institute exhibiting multi-media works by San Diego artists.

Moving south from the Prado's central area is the half-shell Spreckels Outdoor Organ Pavilion, offering free Sunday afternoon concerts.

Finally, in the renovated Ford Motor Co. building, we come to the San Diego Aerospace Museum and International Aerospace Hall of Fame. The circular interior wall mural, painted in 1935 and the largest wall mural in North America, depicts the history of transportation. Over 50 aircraft are on display here including a replica of "The Spirit of St. Louis." The original plane in which Charles Lindbergh crossed the Atlantic was built by Ryan Aircraft in San Diego.

Along with culture, the park pays an equal tribute to nature. On both sides of the 50-year-old Cabrillo Bridge you will find yourself among ancient trees that overshadow grassy arroyos and mesas. Scattered in this greenery are areas for picnicking, lawn bowling, tennis, golf, baseball, and bicycling.

SAN DIEGO ZOO

The San Diego Zoo started inauspiciously in 1916 with a small, rag-tag collection of abandoned animals. For lack of a better location, they were housed on the barren, rugged canyons and mesas of Balboa Park.

Today, all that was barren has been replaced by a lush 128-acre tropical garden, home to 3000 animals representing 800 species. The San Diego Zoo is considered unequalled by any zoo in the world, and valuable as is the animal collection, the botanical collection is estimated to represent an even greater monetary worth.

Designed to delight any age, the zoo's most outstanding achievement has been in creating grottos that closely resemble the animals' natural environments.

WILD ANIMAL PARK

Animals from Africa and Asia roam the 1800 acre
wilds of San Diego's Wild Animal Park at San Pas-
qual where the land closely resembles their native
environment.

Since opening in 1972, the park has become a
haven for several endangered species: Indian and
Northern white rhinos, gorillas, and three creatures
believed to be extinct in their native habitats — the
Arabian oryx, white-tailed gnu, and the Prezwalski
horse.

CORONADO

Coronado embodies much of San Diego's colorful history: Hotel Del Coronado, the magnificent Victorian resort hotel built in the 1880's and recently declared a national historic treasure; North Island Naval Air Station, scene of aviations early development; and the sheltered haven of businesses catering to the wealthy, the retired and the fastidious.

The Hotel Del Coronado is a wooden-wonder from another era that has been lovingly restored. It is here that movie stars, kings, princes, presidents and dignitaries from around the world have played through the generations.

Glenn Curtis established the nation's first flying school on North Island in 1910. The Naval Air Station followed in 1917 and now serves as one of the Navy's largest West Coast repair facilities.

MISSION BEACH

Boasting a two-mile stretch of white sand and well-formed waves, Mission Beach traditionally has been one of the most active and popular beaches in San Diego. Year around residents and summer people mingle on the boardwalk to roller skate, bicycle, skateboard, observe the sailing and surfing or just walk along and people-watch.

Annually, surfing championships draw throngs to watch entrants from around the globe shoot the glassy breakers.

MISSION BAY

Take 4600 acres of irregular swampland, master-plan its development over a 20-year period, raise $50,000,000 for the project, and you will have a feeling for Mission Bay Aquatic Park. Although sprinkled with resort hotels, marinas, restaurants and amusement centers, commercialism is at a minimum: Mission Bay retains a natural relationship with its environment with open beaches, calm water basins and clean salt air.

SEA WORLD

Since its 1964 opening on the shores of Mission Bay, Sea World has been dedicated to presenting the finest quality aquatic entertainment in the world. The company has been so successful in realizing its goal that new parks opened in Ohio and Florida have received the same enthusiastic response from visitors as the original one.

Marine animals in spectacular shows, educational exhibits and aquariums all enhanced by the lush, park-like setting, draws millions of visitors each year.

Here Shamu, the 4700 pound killer whale, demonstrates one of the learned behaviors that keeps both adults and children coming back to Sea World for more.

LA JOLLA

Above spray-drenched cliffs, palatial homes fit snugly on emerald hills. A sheltered cove in the midst of a marine life preserve attracts both sea lions and sunbathers. Tide pools and rock-strewn shores offer interesting finds and formations. "The Village," as La Jollans call their community, is San Diego's Mediterranean spa.

All the amenities of a seaside resort are there, but it is definitely not flashy. Quiet streets, unusual shops and subdued dignity is more the mode.

continued

LA JOLLA *continued*

On the bluffs above the village is San Diego's branch of the University of California, widely noted for its academic excellence and award-winning architecture. Illustrating the latter is the cantilevered UCSD library which has become a tourist attraction in its own right.

Although La Jolla has no industry per se, the concentration of academic and medical facilities has been instrumental in drawing highly sophisticated scientific research and development industries to the surrounding area. The proximity to such institutions as Scripps Institute of Oceanography, Scripps Clinic and Research Foundation and Salk Institute has created a uniquely workable environment of exchange for the scientifically oriented academic and business communities.

Pictured at left is the rim of Torrey Pines Municipal Golf Course, one of over 60 courses scattered throughout San Diego County.

Sunset off La Jolla Shores looking south toward Scripps Pier.

Sail planes and hang-gliders take advantage of wind currents off Torrey Pines State Reserve north of La Jolla. One of the rarest trees in the world, the Torrey Pine now survives in gnarled splendor only in San Diego and on

DEL MAR

This is a charming coastal community widely known for thoroughbred racing. The Del Mar Turf Club, founded by Bing Crosby and Pat O'Brien (among others) opened its gates in 1937 and has held an annual summer meet ever since. The track has always had a comfortably low-key ambience and still attracts Hollywood notables as well as owners, breeders and racing enthusiasts each season.

RANCHO SANTA FE

Horse and rider is a very common scene throughout Rancho Santa Fe. This rambling ranch community, ten minutes east of Del Mar, is said to be one of the most attractive planned residential areas in California, and conceded to be one of the wealthiest. Homesites, mainly planted with citrus, range between 2½ acres to the fabled 800-acre Rancho Zorro where Douglas Fairbanks once lived.

ENCINITAS

Rainbows fill the soft slopes of Encinitas from row-upon-row of brilliantly colored flowers during every season of the year. San Diego County's moderate climate helps to make it one of the most productive commercial flower growing areas of the world.

OCEANSIDE

This pleasant residential seaside community has a beautiful beach and harbor and serves as a distribution center for the productive agricultural section inland.

Oceanside is probably best identified as the site of Camp Pendleton, the largest Marine Corps base in the country. Named after Col. Joseph H. Pendleton, commander of the first marine detachment at San Diego in 1914, Camp Pendleton has trained thousands of young men since its beginning in 1942.

Enhancing Oceanside's modern man-made harbor, Cape Cod Village offers the pleasant diversion of restaurants, gourmet shops and boutiques.

RANCHO BERNARDO

Rancho Bernardo was one of San Diego County's early "new towns," built from scratch on semi-arid grazing land about 30 minutes north and inland of downtown. Conscientious planning created a verdant community complete with green belts, recreational and shopping facilities.

Lured by the subdued setting, industries such as Allstate, Burroughs, National Cash Register and Sony Corporation established branches that architecturally blend and financially contribute to the county's economic base.

The Mercado is a brightly designed shopping center housing restaurants and boutiques popular with residents and as an excursion point for those in surrounding areas.

MOUNT PALOMAR

The white-domed observatory, a giant symbol of man's scientific approach to the heavens, sits among lilac and pine on 6,140 foot Palomar Mountain. Since 1949, astronomers from the California Institute of Technology have been using this site to photographically chart stellar and planetary movement with the Hale telescope. It is noted to have the world's largest reflector, 200 inches, and to be the most delicately balanced — the 530-ton telescope is moved by a 1/12 hp. engine.

Precision and polish dominate this mountain; however, nature's roughhewn elements are all around. Campsites and hiking trails belonging to Palomar Mountain State Park sit below the dome at the 5,300 foot level.

On the way to Palomar Mountain is San Diego County's largest inland body of water, Lake Henshaw. Its 25-mile shoreline and island studded center offer good fishing, camping and sight-seeing.

JULIAN

"Gold!" The cry rang through San Diego in 1869. It came from what was then the second largest town in the County tucked high in the Laguna Mountains. Once a glittering boom town, Julian long-ago settled into a scenic, sleepy community when the color was washed from her streams and picked from her mines.

Julian's lusty history remains as a sampler memory: the original Julian Hotel, built more than 100 years ago by a freed black woman from the South, still offers today's travelers bed and board; the Witch Creek School, started in 1888, has been converted into a library; the Memorial Museum echoes lives and relics of past residents; and the gold is brought *into* town by visitors coming to enjoy the annual apple festival and weed show.

CUYAMACA

Lying peacefully adjacent to Julian, Cuyamaca Rancho State Park's 20,000 wooded acres and sunny meadows provide refuge for people and animals alike. Take a brisk horseback ride . . . feel a trout tug your line . . . throw snowballs in the winter . . . picnic, camp or enjoy a quiet walk. Cuyamaca offers all this and more.

ANZA-BORREGO DESERT STATE PARK

On the surface, the parched lowlands, rough mountains and sheer canyons of Anza-Borrego State Park may seem an arid wasteland. But within its one-half-million acre expanse is a lush and lively wilderness microcosm.

Color fills the desert floor during winter and spring as wildflowers bloom and spiny cactus changes from brown to green with the rainfall. Bighorn sheep, fox, kangaroo rat, antelope, rabbit, mountain lion and mule deer nest and forage in the bracken. More than 150 varieties of birds make their homes among the weeds and willows surrounding the natural springs.

Cohabiting with this wild is Borrego Springs, a resort resting in a 50,000 acre irrigated desert valley. It provides an excellent base for exploring the park while furnishing comfortable accommodations and recreational facilities.

Isolated, yes . . . but never desolate for the true observer of nature. With every turn lies arresting vistas of element-sculptured canyons, time-eroded mountains and the illusive desert floor.

TIJUANA

There are numerous reasons for including Tijuana in a book about San Diego, not the least of which is that it's hard to ignore a city of over 800,000 population living at your doorstep.

continued

Mexico's cultural influence, from food to architecture, is inescapable in the Southwest, and nowhere is it easier to experience first hand. Only 20 minutes from downtown San Diego is the busiest international border gate in the world with over *30 million* people crossing each year.

Shopping at a free port is a major attraction, with perfumes and haute couture fashions at duty free prices leading the list of imported bargains.

Mexico has a thousand year tradition of handcrafts and native arts are still being practiced throughout the country. Silver, articles of papier mache (such as the symbolic tree of life shown in the shop above), leather goods and iron work are popular items purchased by Norteamericanos.

Sports lure many across the border regularly. At Caliente, horses and dogs alternate racing schedules; bullfights at Plaza de Toros and Plaza Monumental draw matadors of world renown; and Jai Alai, reputedly the fastest game in the world, can all be enjoyed by aficionados.

Printed by Frye & Smith